Understanding Your Young Child with Special Needs

Pamela Bartram

Jessica Kingsley Publishers
London and Philadelphia

First published in 2007
by Jessica Kingsley Publishers
116 Pentonville Road
London N1 9JB, UK
and
400 Market Street, Suite 400
Philadelphia, PA 19106, USA

www.jkp.com

Library of Congress Cataloging in Publication Data
A CIP catalog record for this book is available from the Library of Congress

British Library Cataloguing in Publication Data
A CIP catalogue record for this book is available from the British Library

ISBN 978 1 84310 533 6

Printed and bound in Great Britain by
Athenaeum Press, Gateshead, Tyne and Wear

For M, F and J

LEICESTER CITY LIBRARIES	
642	
Bertrams	19.08.07
362.4083	£8.99

Acknowledgement

With grateful thanks to the families and colleagues who help me to understand.

Contents

Foreword

The Tavistock Clinic has an international reputation as a centre of excellence for training, clinical mental health work, research and scholarship. Established in 1920, its history is one of groundbreaking work. The original aim of the Clinic was to offer treatment which could be used as the basis of research into the social prevention and treatment of mental health problems, and to teach these emerging skills to other professionals. Later work turned towards the treatment of trauma, the understanding of conscious and unconscious processes in groups, as well as important and influential work in developmental psychology. Work in perinatal bereavement led to a new understanding within the medical profession of the experience of stillbirth, and of the development of new forms of support for mourning parents and families. The development in the 1950s and 1960s of a systemic model of psychotherapy, focusing on the interaction between children and parents and within families, has grown into the substantial body of theoretical knowledge and therapeutic techniques used in the Tavistock's training and research in family therapy.

The Understanding Your Child series has an important place in the history of the Tavistock Clinic. It has been issued in a completely new form three times: in the 1960s, the 1990s, and in 2004. Each time the authors, drawing on their clinical background and specialist training, have set out to reflect on the extraordinary story of "ordinary development" as it was observed and experienced at the time. Society changes, of course, and so has this series, as it attempts to make sense of everyday accounts of the ways in which a developing child interacts with his or her parents, carers and the wider world. But within this changing scene there has been something constant, and it is best described as a continuing enthusiasm for a view of development which recognizes the importance of the strong feelings and emotions experienced at each stage of development.

The context of this very important book is both the world of special needs, and developmental progress. The author, Pamela Bartram, describes in a moving way the themes of ordinary developmental progress within the particular challenge of special needs. There are many powerful examples in the book, and these are thrown into relief by a knowledgeable and sympathetic commentary. The various chapters consider the complex nature of emotional bonds in such situations,and explore the issues common to all parents, such as managing sibling relationships, toilet training and behaviour, as well as those issues particular to parents of a child with special needs, including dealing with diagnosis and the stresses on family relations.

Pamela Bartram offers insights that will provide advice and food for thought for parents and professionals working with families.

Jonathan Bradley
Child Psychotherapist
General Editor of the Understanding Your Child series

Introduction

This book is primarily for parents, although it will also be helpful to any professionals working with babies and pre-school children with special needs. As such, when addressing the reader, it can be assumed that I am addressing parents. The area of special needs brings many parents into contact with a range of professionals, in health, mental health, education, social services and the voluntary sector. At times, I will address the interest of professionals specifically.

The title suggests an intention to inform parents about how to understand their child with special needs and this requires some qualification.

First, as this book is about children, much of it will, of necessity, focus on the ordinariness and not the "special-ness" of the child. In this I hope to counteract a common tendency to focus on disability and special needs at the expense of thinking about the individual child – her personality, family life and the feelings and behaviour which are part of her normal developmental processes. However, I will try to hold a balance between thinking about the tasks and challenges of "ordinary" parenting and those specific to the parents of the young child with special needs. This balancing act mirrors that which parents of young children with special needs have to attempt much of the time.

The second qualification stems from my belief that most parents already have a deep connection with and therefore understanding of their young child with special needs. Nevertheless, their confidence in their own understanding and responses is vulnerable to disruption by factors which come along with the special needs themselves. It can easily appear that other people have the expertise about the child, rather than parents themselves being the experts. One mother ruefully admitted she imagined someone else has "a secret store of answers" to which she wished to gain access! I do not wish to add weight to that idea. I hope, therefore, that intertwined with my own voice, the voices of parents who bring up children with special needs will come through, bringing to this account their knowledge and experience.

The third qualification has to do with the inherent challenge of understanding babies and small children whose minds or bodies are handicapped, to varying degrees, by disability. Just as it is hard for them both to express themselves and make sense of the world, so is it an ambitious task for us to make sense of their experience. An account of children with special needs would be a poor one if it did not acknowledge that inevitably, we sometimes reach the limits of our understanding. Yet in order to feel a properly human connection with the children and with each other as we care for them, we must try to understand.

This book, like the others in the series, is written from a psychoanalytic viewpoint and values the idea, therefore, that powerful feelings and unwanted thoughts, when unacknowledged, can throw spanners in the work of our relationships and endeavours. A fundamental tenet of psychoanalysis is that the more we are able to understand ourselves, the better we can hope to understand and communicate with others. This entails having time and space to notice and reflect on what we are experiencing. That kind of understanding is not the same as the acquisition of facts about conditions. To acknowledge its importance is to emphasize the deeply personal and inherently emotional nature of the complex bonds between self and others and especially between parent and child.

In my experience of working with the parents of young children who have special needs there can be many obstacles which get in the way of this self-reflective activity. Some obstacles are practical, to do with the pressure of the everyday demands associated with a child's special needs. Others have their origins in feelings, especially the fear of being overwhelmed by difficult and frightening feelings. Often there is a mixture of the two.

> One mother of a child recently diagnosed with a severely disabling condition told me she dare not stop and think too long about her feelings. "There are so many appointments to attend, forms to fill in and my other child to care for, I'm afraid that if I start to think about what I am feeling I won't be able to keep going."

There is a very personal balance to be struck between persevering with the job of parenting, sometimes described by parents of children with special needs in terms of "battling to keep going", and stopping to reflect on your predicament and its impact on you. Families as well as the individuals in them have different ways of managing. However, the depth of parents' relationships with and understanding of their children can be enriched by having the opportunity to understand their own assumptions about as well as their contributions and reactions to their children. This in turn leads to a sense of greater well-being.

This book therefore is not a vehicle for giving instruction or advice. It is, rather, an attempt to reflect on the experience of parenting a young child with special needs, informed by an understanding of child development and of the emotional states of parents and children. I hope this process will free you the reader to find creative ways of parenting which are individual to you and to which you feel emotionally connected.

A final note on the vexed subject of terminology. My colleague, the child psychotherapist and psychoanalyst Valerie Sinason, often commented on how problematic is the terminology of disability. It appears that no words or phrases remain acceptable in our culture for long, no doubt a symptom of our deeper difficulty in living with disability and all it conjures for us. Valerie Sinason's first version of this book, published in 1993, was entitled *Understanding Your Handicapped Child*, a title which only fourteen years later seems out of date. "Spastic", "Learning Disabled" and "Mentally Handicapped" have all in their turn given way to new terms which for a while seem more acceptable until they too are one day deemed offensive and in need of replacement. As one author puts it, "Old meanings infect new words" (Stoller 1985, p.5).

> One mother told me with feeling that she hates to hear her child described as a "special needs child". She felt he should be described as "a child with special needs". To her, this distinction was very important, emphasizing as it does, first the child and only second the special needs.

Even now, the term "special needs" will in turn give way to new phrases. For the time being, however, I hope readers will accept my use of the terms "child with special needs" or "child with a disability", with the assurance that they are intended neither to denigrate nor to offend.

All of the stories in this book are based on encounters with real children and their families. However, their identities are disguised to protect their privacy. I will refer to "he" and "she" throughout, with no particular criteria for the use of one form rather than another.

1

Expectations and Birth

Pregnancy

Parents' relationship with their baby starts long before they hold her for the first time. Even before conception, thoughts and feelings about the baby they will have one day may form part of the parents' inner world into which the baby arrives. The baby-to-be may be associated in their mind with a relative, perhaps a beloved parent. In some cultures it is still common practice to name babies after a grandparent or other relative. This can be full of meaning, sometimes expressing the wish to make a link across generations or to see the continuing existence in the child of the best qualities of the relative. A special case of this is when a planned baby is associated in parents' minds with a family member who has died, a particularly powerful situation where many feelings, hopes and expectations may be placed on the new life.

As a pregnancy progresses the connection between parent and child develops. The mother is physically close to the baby and begins to have more conscious ideas about what sort of baby she is carrying. Modern medical practices such as routine scans reinforce parents' sense of knowing their baby. They may have a photograph of the scanned image – their first sight of their new child.

A new baby represents a new start. We may wish to pass on to our child the good experiences we have had as children or do things differently from our parents and give our children a better experience than our own. Whatever the case, a new life symbolizes new hope and new possibilities.

Pregnancy also puts parents in touch with how precious and precarious life is. The vulnerability of the foetus, completely dependent for his well-being on the mother who carries him, is something we may be more or less consciously aware of.

> When asked whether she would prefer a boy or a girl, Janet gave a response typical of many expectant mothers. "As long as it has all its fingers and toes, I will be happy."

This is a way of alluding to the possibility of ill health or disability, the unwelcome outcome of a pregnancy. Whereas some expectant parents will think and talk about this possibility openly, for others it is a topic to avoid, almost as if to discuss it would be to invite bad luck.

When a baby arrives who has severe health problems or a disability, therefore, the emotional impact on parents has to be understood in the context of all the ordinary hopes and fantasies which had gathered around the idea of the baby even before conception. This is inescapable.

"Welcome to Holland"

Several parents have drawn my attention to a piece of writing by Emily Perl Kingsley, the mother of a child with special needs. They say how accurately it captures their own experience. In the article, the writer compares her expectation of the birth of her baby with getting on a plane in anticipation of a wonderful holiday in Italy. However, when she arrives she finds she is in Holland, not Italy. It's not, as she says, as if Holland is a terrible place, just that she was prepared for Italy and all its characteristic delights.

> But everyone you know is busy coming and going from Italy…and they're all bragging about what a wonderful time they had there. And for the rest of your life, you will say "Yes, that's where I was supposed to go. That's what I had planned."
>
> And the pain of that will never, ever, ever, *ever* go away…because the loss of that dream is a very very significant loss.
>
> But…if you spend your life mourning the fact that you didn't get to Italy, you may never be free to enjoy the very special, the very lovely things…about Holland.
>
> *From "Welcome to Holland", reproduced with*
> *permission from Emily Perl Kingsley*

For many parents this seems to captures something central to their experience: the shock of arriving "in Holland"; the gradual process of adjustment to the change of plan; the eventual enjoyment and appreciation of the unanticipated destination; and alongside these feelings, the painful and permanent sense of loss. Emily Perl Kingsley's "Welcome to Holland" is reprinted in full on pp.70–1.

Shock and trauma at the time of birth

It is a sad fact that many parents of special needs children have had a traumatic birth experience. Feelings about the birth can go on to have an impact on what comes afterwards. Yet I am often surprised to find that many parents have been so busy getting on with what needs to be done, they have had neither time nor space emotionally to digest the impact on them of events around the time of the birth.

> One mother described her daughter as "white as marble" when she was born. Doctors took her away and although she knew something was wrong she didn't know what. She thought her baby had died. This image of lifelessness stayed with her and sometimes made it difficult for her to see the lively little girl her daughter was growing into.

It is often the feelings of helplessness which vividly stay with parents. Their own family circumstances may accentuate these feelings.

> Maria wept as she told me about the birth of her child with special needs four years earlier. She and her husband were political refugees in Britain and spoke little English. As the labour with this, their first child, progressed, Maria was in great pain. Unconfident about their spoken English both she and her husband felt helpless to communicate with hospital staff. When the baby was born he had suffered from lack of oxygen in the late stages of labour.

Remembering the sense of helplessness and reliving the panic surrounding her son's birth when he was rushed away from her was distressing for Maria. Her account was as vivid as if the events she was describing had happened not four years previously but yesterday. However, talking about it proved a useful way of leaving the experience in the past. It freed Maria to feel empowered as she continued to look for the best possible help and resources for her son.

Alongside feelings of helplessness are often powerful feelings of guilt. It seems that parents have a deeply in-built belief that they ought to be able to protect their child from harm. When trauma and disability challenge this belief, they are left with a dose of guilt which may be hard to digest.

Films of normal births of ordinary babies reveal patterns in how parents begin to acquaint themselves with their new baby (Macfarlane 1977). They make an "inventory" of parts of the baby's body and comment on the likeness of the baby to another family member, often the father. In this way emotional bonds are strengthened between the couple and with the new arrival. By contrast with this, the arrival of a baby with a complex disability, perhaps involving physical disfigurement, can be a frightening experience. The child may need to be taken away urgently by the doctors and nurses, perhaps for a life-saving intervention. The ordinary early experiences of taking in the new baby are not available to parents under those circumstances. This may be the first, but probably not the last, experience of feeling that the professionals and not the parents have the expertise the baby needs.

Prematurity

A major change in the ability of the medical professions to keep younger premature babies alive has resulted in more babies surviving prematurely. While some pre-term babies can go on to make surprisingly good progress, others may have medical problems or brain damage from which they cannot recover.

> Cathy reported her experience of watching her tiny pre-term baby being subject to many painful medical interventions, unable to pick her up, unable to make her voice heard above the noise of whirring machines. When I asked her what she remembered most vividly about her daughter's many months in hospital, she said "fear". She asked me anxiously whether her daughter, who in fact made very good medical and developmental progress, would suffer from her memories of those early experiences.

> Joanne, mother of a baby born at 24 weeks' gestation, started a playgroup for former premature babies because she knew from her own experience how difficult it was to take her child along to ordinary playgroups where the other children were larger and more robust. In a leaflet for other parents, she wrote of her experience when her daughter was in special care: "I was terrified that she would die at any moment, while I was there watching her and at the same time horrified at the thought that she might die while I was not there."

Many parents vividly convey their acute mental and emotional alertness at that time of their baby's birth; they experienced a state of mind in which their whole being was caught up with the baby's life, often balanced between survival and death. As in other life crises, in these emotional states, energy is somehow found when it is needed. However, as the external situation changes, it can be difficult to leave behind or grow out of those states of mind. They may continue to exert an influence on the parent even when they have outlived their usefulness.

> The mother of Lewis, a seven-year-old boy, talked of her vigil in the special care baby unit when her son was born at 26 weeks' gestation. She described movingly how she sat by his incubator day and night. She firmly believed that if she took her eyes off him for any length of time he would die. She believed that quite literally her "regard" for him had kept him alive. When I met her several years later, her son had made very good progress and doctors commented that he had done surprisingly well. However, mother and son were still having difficulties in separating which could be seen in their sleeping habits and in the boy's reluctance to attend school.

> Baby Sean was also born at 24 weeks' gestation. Sadly his young mother, a drug addict, did not visit him in the special care baby unit. He was tended to by the nurses, who noticed how restless he was and how hard to comfort when distressed. The impact on him of the drugs his mother took was important in terms of his physical condition. In addition to this, he did not have the consistency of one person attending to him.

The psychoanalyst William Bion writes about the importance of "maternal reverie" for the emotional well-being of a baby (Bion 1984, Chapter 12). By this he refers to the caregiver's ability to present the baby with a mental and emotional space to fill. The ability to make a space inside your own mind in which to absorb the impact of the baby on you provides a psychological holding which goes along with and parallels the physical holding such premature babies are now found to thrive on. In the practice of "kangarooing" it is found that the premature babies held in close proximity on the chest of mother or father benefit in many ways from that intimate physical contact (Wahlberg, Alfonso and Persson 1992).

It is hard for us to know what these experiences, shocking for parents, are like for the babies themselves. We know that babies feel pain and that pain is stressful for babies as it is for children and adults.

> One little girl, brain damaged at birth, used to sing the Humpty Dumpty nursery rhyme over and over. Her mother suggested to me that perhaps somewhere she was aware of the great "fall" she had had. Perhaps she was expressing her fear that like Humpty Dumpty, she too could never be "put back together again". This was of course a very painful thought, and it took courage on the part of her mother to think it.

> Another boy, Sam, was described by the occupational therapist as having "sensory integration" difficulties. These are difficulties in sorting out and interpreting information that comes through the senses and so affect the child's physical and sensory experience of the world. Sam's parents reflected that his operations, many injections and tube feeding as a small baby may well have interfered with the development of his ability to discern and discriminate physical experiences in an ordinary way.

Antidotes

Sigmund Freud adopted the term "trauma" from the Greek word which means "to pierce". The birth experiences I have been describing were to a degree traumatic, threatening temporarily to disturb the equilibrium of the parents' state of mind, or pierce the psychic skin which most of the time successfully contains our subjective experience.

There are factors which, however, can act as antidotes to trauma, mitigating the intensity and duration of its effects. Without such antidotes, feelings of helplessness and attendant guilt experienced at birth can continue to exert a powerful influence, undermining parents' sense of themselves as the rightful centre of their baby's world.

A well-established and solid sense of internal security in part stemming from parents' own childhood experiences is one such antidote. The ability to access this helpful internal resource will help them bear the brunt of the frightening threat of their world falling apart.

Good bonds with family and close friends and a supportive partnership are other factors which strengthen parents when they find themselves shocked and in pain. Religious faith may also support their natural attempts to make sense of the arrival of a baby with special needs. *I*

> Hassam was the fourth child of a mother from North Africa. He was born with a genetically transmitted condition affecting his sight and he was unable to feed by sucking so a gastrostomy tube was fitted. A visit when he was two weeks old found his mother sitting by his cot where he lay sleeping. As she spoke to the visitor about his problems she wept openly. Her own mother, who spoke no English, was visiting from their home country. She nodded and wept with her daughter. Hassam's movements became more agitated and he began to cry, first little sounds, gradually building up in a crescendo. He moved his head from side to side. Mother spoke to him gently, telling him in her own language that she could hear him. She stroked his tummy and touched his hand and he quietened briefly before beginning to cry again. She reached into the cot and picked him up, supporting his body until she could bring it into contact with hers and hold him against her chest. Hassam's crying gradually subsided. Mother talked rhythmically to him rocking her own body gently so he was also rocked with her. She wiped her tears away with the back of her hand and went on speaking to him. Her own mother watched them, weeping silently.

Hassam's mother had a powerful capacity to experience her feelings deeply, without being completely overwhelmed. Although it might appear paradoxical, this capacity seems to be another antidote to the potentially damaging effects of psychological shock and hurt.

2

Getting Together

Getting together

The developmental psychologist and psychoanalyst, Daniel Stern, writes about "the mother–infant dance" (Stern 1977, p.145). With this image he draws attention to exchanges between a parent and a baby which are natural, pre-verbal and profoundly based in rhythm, pitch, tone and timbre, the non-verbal aspects of human communication. These exchanges do not take place just at "playtime". If you watch a baby being fed by breast or bottle you can discern the wordless, rhythmic nature of the experience, as parent and child "get into step" with each other and share an ordinary yet intimate and essential experience, the foundation of their developing relationship.

During mealtimes, for example, when an older baby is being spoon fed, observation shows that much of the experience is mediated through rhythms shared between baby and parent with no conscious effort on the parent's part. Musicians and psychologists who have analysed videotape of these exchanges have demonstrated that babies and their parents instinctively synchronize their actions and vocalizations long before words carry meaning for the baby. These shared experiences of physical and sensory attunement are central to the baby's sense of well-being. The baby has repeated experiences of being "met up with" physically and psychologically, of her experiences being shareable and shared.

This is not to say that everything that happens between a parent and a baby has to be so perfectly timed and judged that no dissonance or arrhythmia (out-of-step-ness) ever occurs. Indeed it is also part of ordinary experience that exchanges are at times out of step. The baby's experience of finding that such moments are part of ordinary life is also important. What matters is not that exchanges should always be "right" but that the pair, whether mother and baby or father and baby, can continue to have an impact on each other. Between them they go on finding satisfying and constructive exchanges, while integrating the experience of "overshoots" or mismatches in a lively and flexible way. Smell, touch, sound and sight all mediate these processes.

Hassam and his mother, described at the end of Chapter 1, were seen negotiating together his waves of feeling. They were able to communicate, or perhaps more accurately, *commune* with each other; to share the dance in a way which encompassed both his disability and the depth of her feelings for him.

Empathy

Empathy is the ability to put yourself in someone else's shoes and ask what the world looks and feels like from there. It is an important factor in all human relationships and especially in parenting. In normal development the parent tells herself a story about the baby's experience. Parents create stories about their baby, a story modified, when all goes well by their changing daily experience of that individual child.

The capacity for both "reverie" described in Chapter 1 and empathy are important for the kind of attunement which enables the parent–infant dance to unfold.

When a baby is born with special needs, these natural processes are placed under great strain. Parents may be unsure how to interpret the baby, and lack confidence to make a narrative about him which includes his emotional life as well as ideas about his level of understanding. They may be unsure how much of a person he is.

Is the baby's physical unsettledness to do with his brain, his difficulty in processing sensory information? Perhaps it has to do with his experience of a difficult birth or medical interventions, or his physical condition. Does she feel uncomfortable? Is she in pain, hungry or tired? Perhaps she is feeling unhappy and lonely as any baby does sometimes.

Sadly for some babies, even those without special needs, their parents are not able to attune to them or empathize with them in the ways described. This may be because the parent's mind is too much elsewhere, preoccupied by grief or consumed by other strong feelings. The parent may be unduly full of anger or hostility which interferes with the responsiveness needed for parenting. When this happens, the baby's physiological experience and psychological development is affected. It is in the light of this that the complex task of parenting a baby with special needs has to be understood.

Babies with special needs

What happens then when a baby is born with a disability? To understand your child's experience is certainly a much more complicated task for parents where there are special needs. It is particularly challenging to put yourself in the shoes of a small baby who is having to go through painful procedures, hard to know your child is experiencing a pain or discomfort which you cannot alleviate and human to resist acknowledging it to yourself.

The delicate process of getting together can be disrupted early on by events such as emergency medical intervention at birth or the shock of diagnosis. It is important that the training of hospital staff helps them to manage these difficult situations sensitively. One way of approaching this is to help them to acknowledge the emotional impact of these events on themselves as well as on parents.

There are also practical matters to consider. If the baby is blind, for example, the exchange of loving gazes will not be part of their shared repertoire. Through other senses, however, she can nevertheless sense her parents' attunement to her physiological states and her moods.

> Joelle was born blind. She had a limited range of facial expressions with which to convey her moods and feelings. This made it difficult for her parents to read her expressions as they had been able to do with ease when dealing with her older sister. Instinctively, they paid more attention to her bodily movements. How relaxed or tense did her body feel? Was she straining one way to listen carefully to a sound? By their following her lead and focusing on how she could communicate she developed a secure sense of herself as a communicator.

> Matthew, a first baby, was born with multiple physical problems following a trouble-free pregnancy. By contrast with Joelle's parents, Matthew's mother found it difficult to get together with him and felt the task would be managed more expertly by someone from outside the family who had previous experience of babies with special needs. Matthew's father and mother quickly engaged a nanny who they felt knew much more than they did about looking after his special needs. Mother threw herself into her work more quickly than she had

planned. It took several months for Mother, with Father's support, to recover from the shock of having a baby with so many special needs and begin to regain her confidence. She was convinced that she did not "have the skills" to look after a baby with special needs.

Developments in brain research

In some cases, parents find it difficult to believe that what they do in these early stages of their baby's development can make a difference when their baby so clearly has significant physical difficulties. However, developments in our understanding of babies' brain development shows that this is far from the case.

In her book *Why Love Matters: How Affection Shapes a Baby's Brain* (2004), Sue Gerhardt describes what she calls "the corrosive effect" on brain development of cortisol, a hormone produced by the body as a response to stress (Gerhardt 2004, pp.56). Extra cortisol is created as a way of focusing the individual's energy on coping with the stressful situation and is therefore helpful in the short term. However:

> The cortisol puts brakes on the immune system, the capacity to learn and to relax... If the stress goes on for a very long time you might get forgetful as the hippocampus is central to learning and memory... As the saying goes..."Stress makes you stupid". (Gerhardt 2004, pp.61–2)

These insights have implications for babies with special needs and their parents. Both are likely to experience more stress than the average baby and its parent. The baby may be in pain or discomfort because of his condition or additionally because of the medical and therapeutic interventions he has to go through. Sensory sensitivities and difficulties in taking in and processing information about the world around her may add to the stress experienced. In turn, the parents may be struggling with tiredness and anxiety in their own right as well as going through the baby's difficult experiences as it were "by proxy".

Sue Gerhardt goes on to explain that small babies who are touched and held can cope better with cortisol produced by stressful experiences, by developing something called "cortisol receptors" in their brain.

Through this research into brain development we can see how it is that early care "shapes the developing nervous system and determines how stress is interpreted and responded to in the future" (Gerhardt 2004, p.64). Some babies born after a traumatic birth and post-birth experience are highly reactive; that is, difficult to soothe and out-of-kilter. They may be, therefore, even more vulnerable to the effects of further stress.

Some parents' concern that nothing they can do will make the situation better is likely to be far from the case. They find that while their own resources are severely tested, at the same time they need to find extra with which to help their baby to manage. It is not a surprise that caring for a baby or young child with special needs is such a demanding job.

The baby with special needs may take longer than an ordinary baby to show you he knows you are there.

Babies with cerebral palsy can be particularly hard to calm and settle.

> Rhiannon was born with cerebral palsy as a result of lack of oxygen at birth. She cried a high-pitched cry for what her mother described as "days on end" and her parents could find no way of settling her. She slept for short bursts and would waken, already crying. Her mother said it wasn't the cerebral palsy which was so difficult to live with. But to have a baby you cannot "get through to" or comfort was what made her despair. With patient handling and good support from family and professionals, Rhiannon became more settled. She started to turn to her mother's voice, smile and gaze at her mother, father and brother after several months of relative unresponsiveness. This was an important turning point for the family. As her father said, "At last she is here".

Signs of autism in the first year of life

New developments in studies of children with autism reveal that early signs of autism, or "red flags" as they are sometimes described, can be detected in some cases in the first few months of life. Some of this important work has been done by studying family videos of identical twins, one of whom went on to be diagnosed with autism. It has been possible to detect differences in the motor movements of these children from their twins, as well as subtle impairments in their expression of feelings and social behaviour (Acquarone 2007).

What is of great importance in these studies is that although parents have not consciously detected any problems in the twin with difficulties, in subtle ways they have adapted the way that they relate to the impaired twin. This is expressed through, for example the intonation of their voice, and the way they address the baby, which differ from how they speak to the normally developing twin.

This shows the subtle and close awareness between parents and their babies which occurs quite unconsciously. However, it also indicates the possibility of patterns of relating becoming reinforced without being properly aware, as children with difficulties in getting together with their parents may not be exposed to the same influences as their normal siblings. This important area of study opens up the possibility of much earlier intervention for these children, and earlier support for parents, to prevent unsatisfactory patterns of relating from becoming established at an early stage of development.

3

Letting Go

Sleep and sleeplessness

Families where there is a child with a disability are more prone to sleep problems than other families. This may be for a number of reasons, some physical and others psychological or social. Some children, for example, may need nursing interventions or medication during the night. A child with muscular contractions or hypertonia (increased muscle tone) may be unable to move around in bed at night in the normal way and so is awakened by discomfort and distress and unable to soothe herself. A baby who has had a difficult start in life is more likely to feel insecure when separated from her parents, alone in the dark at night-time. Parents may have had frightening experiences of seeing their child stop breathing, or having convulsions.

All of these factors can contribute to a sleep difficulty which in turn has an impact on the whole of family life. Family conflict, depression or even marital breakdown can result from long periods of sleep disruption. Parents' capacity to hold on to their jobs is also likely to be affected with attendant impact on parents' sense of agency and economic status.

Parents of course have to manage the physical risks, if any, to their young child at night. Sometimes, however, as in Lewis' case (page 19) it is hard for parents to believe that the life-or-death situation their child was in at one point is now in the past, even when this is in fact the case. Despite parents' best intentions, they may contribute to the sleep difficulty by being overly responsive to the child's request for company at night.

Giving your child the affection or reassurance he needs, ensuring his physical safety and comfort as much as possible, while also reassuring him that he can manage without you, is almost an impossible balance to achieve.

The process of settling a child at night may take longer than when matters are more straightforward.

In some circumstances night-time separations are even further complicated by parents' experience before the baby was born.

> Jenny, aged four, has cerebral palsy affecting all her limbs. Her sleep was constantly disturbed at night and her crying several times a night awoke her parents. They had taken to sleeping separately in order to take turns looking after Jenny so that one of them could get a good night's sleep. Jenny had convulsions during the first two years of her life but they had since stopped. Her anti-epileptic medication seemed to be working well. The occupational therapist provided a special mattress so that she had more freedom and comfort in bed. Still, however, she woke several times a night, calling out for her mother or father and angrily rejecting the parent who arrived if it was not the one called for! Jenny's mother could not imagine a time when Jenny would sleep through the night. In fact several years before, another baby in the family had suffered a cot death. When this was explored with Jenny's parents, they could see that their fears for Jenny's life were stopping them from giving her a clear message about what she needed to do at night-time.

There can be other reasons for feeling unsure about how to approach sleep difficulties in a young child.

> Lara, aged two, had come for an assessment because her parents thought she might be autistic. They had three older children and had already successfully negotiated many stages of normal development with them. Lara's mother told me how exhausted she was. Lara would not settle at night. Unlike her practice with the older children, when Lara woke at night, she allowed her to get up and roam around the house. Sometimes she, her husband and Lara were awake for hours on end. Mother was pale and exhausted, unlike Lara, who caught up on sleep during the day, taking long naps! When I asked her whether she had thought of changing these habits, she told me that she was waiting for the diagnosis before doing so. If Lara was autistic, then she would need to know that. It would change her approach to the problem of sleep. Puzzled by this, I asked why Lara's mother was not taking any action. She told me she just felt that the diagnosis would make a difference.

It seemed that while on the one hand Lara's parents longed for sleep, other, perhaps less obvious considerations were also at play. Something, perhaps an intense but not fully conscious sense of protectiveness towards Lara, stopped them from giving her a clear message about night-time. Unfortunately, this created a situation in which Lara did as she wanted, unchallenged. This was not good for her, her parents or for her siblings, who could not understand why she was allowed so much licence.

Of course many young autistic children sleep very badly and some families benefit from behaviour modification programmes or drugs such as melatonin (which occurs naturally in the pigment of the skin) to regulate sleep patterns. In some situations, stronger sedative medication may be prescribed. However, in Lara's case, what was so striking was that her mother and father were not even trying the approaches they had used successfully with their other children. In my experience, when sleep problems are thoughtfully understood and consistently handled, even the sleep difficulties of young autistic children can improve significantly.

> Lara was given a diagnosis of autism. For a while, this diagnosis over-shadowed her parents' ambition for her to sleep well in her own bed. They took her into their bed at night and there was some improvement in her hours of sleeping. After a few months, when they had regained some strength and optimism, they began to think about a sleep programme for getting her back into her own bed.

Threesomes and sleep problems

In the course of normal development, often between two and three years of age, children become intensely curious about the relationship between their parents. This includes curiosity about what goes on between Mummy and Daddy when the child is elsewhere and nowhere is this a more provoking issue than at night in the dark. At that stage of development, the child has to be able to manage the fact and the feelings associated with it, that sometimes he is excluded from what goes on between his parents. He may well feel left out, lonely and jealous. This is an emotional challenge which the child may react to by trying to intrude on the privacy of that relationship.

Children who have been sleeping quite well until this point may become wakeful at night and often come to the parents' bed, with the often uncon-scious intention of seeing and possibly interrupting what is going on. Children who are not mobile may interrupt parents at night by calling out or crying. Even when the parent is single, a young child will still have these worries and ideas which can be linked in their minds with the thought of being displaced or replaced by a new baby coming along.

Many children with special needs may be as susceptible to these worries as other children. Because their intellectual development is delayed, this phase of development may come later than normal. However, it is likely that these ideas and feelings will play a part in sleep difficulties at some point. Having an awareness of these issues will affect how parents talk to a sleepless child, what reassurance they offer them, and to what extent they feel the need to allow the child to, sometimes literally, "get between them" during the night.

It is not always easy for parents of children with special needs to "take the long view", a helpful stance in parenting. This can be because of the lifelong nature of the disability itself. Particularly acute difficulties associated with the process of separation within families where there is a young child with special needs may also play a part. The shadow of the future, where their child remains unable to live independently, may fall over the present.

Parents may not have access to the reassuring thought that "he will grow out of it" or "when he has his first girlfriend he won't still be sleeping in our bed". That future may not be imaginable for them.

Babysitters

Parents of children with a disability are especially vulnerable to social isolation and marital break-up. Finding a babysitter who understands the child's physical needs or strange behaviour is more difficult than finding an ordinary babysitter. However, in some cases the reasons for not having a babysitter and going out are more complex.

> Jack, aged three, was born with Down's syndrome. He was physically well and making good progress in all areas of his development. His parents told me they had not been out together since Jack was born and they could not leave him with the usual babysitter who had cared for their other children. Instead they took turns going out with their friends separately. After getting to know them better, I began to sense that they felt they didn't deserve the right to be a couple again. I wondered if they were afraid, not of each other, but of what might happen between them if they got together intimately. They felt that something might go wrong again if they were truly a couple.

Playgroups

In the early stages of development a child's parents or main carers are his whole world. Gradually this world widens out to include other family members, friends and, let us hope, one day, friends of their own. When a child has a disability this process may naturally take more time. It is important that parents give themselves the opportunity to weigh up thoughtfully the practical demands of work and financial need, against the slow pace of the baby's development.

When a baby is relatively unresponsive and uncommunicative, a mother may long to get back to work where her efforts will be rewarded and her results recognized. Other mothers of children with special needs stay at home and find that life becomes a daily round of medical and therapy appointments.

In some cases, facing the outside world where playgroups and coffee mornings are filled with "normal" children becomes almost impossible and carers hide away at home, so that the child too misses out on developmentally useful experiences.

> One mother told me her friends were organizing a shared care arrangement for babies all born around the same time. She did not feel she could take part because the other mothers would feel awkward and embarrassed that their children were developing normally while her little girl was not. She felt she had to spare them those awkward feelings.

Groups arranged for children with special needs and their carers do not always solve the problem of painful comparisons. Parents may be acutely sensitive to the degree of impairment in their child compared with that of another.

It is also unrealistic to think that parents will make friends with other parents just because they both have a child with special needs. Although they will have some things in common, it may be that without the shared circumstance of having a child with special needs, their paths would never have crossed.

All of these considerations highlight the parents' vulnerability to finding themselves socially isolated and experiencing their job as caregiver as lonely. In turn this can lead to difficulties believing that anyone else can help or share the task, even when an opportunity arises for this.

Nevertheless, the children may well benefit from the company of others, at the early stages, with their carer present.

Nursery and school

Starting nursery or school is an important milestone in the life of a child. The parent of the child with special needs may have complex feelings when the time arises for their child to attend nursery or school. This may be the first time of separation. To leave your child in the care of others when the child is not able to tell you what happened in your absence is a situation which can lead to considerable anxiety.

Issues of mainstream or special school can be difficult for parents to decide on. Both options have their appeal but also their drawbacks. There are concerns that a child's differences will be overlooked or inadequately met in mainstream schools. The idea that a child, although in a mainstream school, may nevertheless be isolated and perhaps even bullied is a painful one to contemplate.

Parents hope there will be more expertise in specialist nurseries and schools. Yet at the same time parents may well worry about the effect on their child of mixing only with other children with special needs.

> Rory's father used a sporting analogy to express this concern, telling me that if you want to play football well you have to play with people who are better than you, not at your own standard.

Young autistic children in particular may not be sociable. Parents worry that if their child mixes only with other unsociable children he will not learn to make friends. Having to make a decision and weigh up these considerations makes the transition into nursery or school an emotionally charged one and reawakens feelings which may have prevailed earlier in the child's life. Just as parents have grown more used to and confident with their child, they have to contemplate entrusting him to staff, sometimes for many hours a day.

Some parents feel that their young child with special needs should be in nursery all day in order to benefit from the stimulation available there. Others feel that because their child is developmentally delayed, she would benefit from having more time at home, rather than less time there.

Parents who opt for mainstream school will need to feel reassured that there will be specialist equipment and other resources available for their children and currently this sometimes involves requesting an assessment of their child's special educational needs by the local education authority. This can become an emotive process in which the education authority is sometimes seen as withholding resources from the child, a very upsetting thought for the family. Here as in other settings, there is a fine line between standing up for your child so that she is given the best possible chance of doing well while away from her family, and becoming locked into "battling", which drains energy and causes great distress.

4

Boundaries and Behaviour

Toilet-training in normal development

In the course of normal development babies and young children become increasingly civilised as they grow and develop within social situations. Toilet-training is an excellent example of this process. During that process, the infant at first has a physical experience of relief or the re-establishing of physical comfort, with the emptying of bladder or bowel. However, this is not an intentional act. The baby certainly has no idea about where the wee or pooh goes once it has left his body. He has little idea of the impact of his evacuations on those around him and no sense of wishing to please someone by doing what is expected, or socially acceptable. The way he is handled physically during a nappy change will have a cumulative impact on him through actions repeated over and over again. One child may be given the message that he is a very clever boy indeed for filling a nappy so well, while another might pick up verbal and non-verbal clues which indicate that nappy changing is an unwelcome chore for the carer.

As children develop neurologically and physiologically, the capacity to monitor and control their evacuations develops. In parallel with this physical process, psychological development also has to take place. The child has to have the ability to understand, conveyed through language, that now his parents would like him to put his pooh and wee in a particular place. Equally importantly he has to want to do what his parents want him to do! That is, from an emotional point of view, he has to want to conform to his parents' wishes in order to please them. We could say that this conforming is an expression of his love for them which has to be able to outweigh any aggressive, antisocial feelings he has towards them.

The child does not go through these stages of development in a vacuum. On the contrary, his parents' feelings and expectations have a crucial part to play. This is also the case where children have special needs.

> Riley, aged four, was severely delayed in all areas of his development. As a tiny baby he had many operations and medical interventions. From a sensory point of view he was under-responsive in some areas, and hyper-responsive in others. His nervous system was disordered and chaotic. His parents reported that although he used the potty to wee in, he always poohed on the floor. Sometimes he went further and smeared the pooh on the walls. They felt that perhaps he could not feel the pooh coming, or else did not understand that pooh goes in the potty. They went on wiping the walls in a resigned way!
>
> Closer observation revealed that Riley would consistently get off the potty in order to pooh on the floor. We began to think that this might not simply be a question either of not knowing what he was about to do, or not understanding that he should pooh in the potty. Once his parents were clearer about this, they conveyed to him in a very straightforward way, their expectation that he use the potty. Some battles of will ensued. After a period of time, longer than for a normally developing child, in which they kept up their efforts, Riley started to use the potty for poohs as well as wees.

With a normally developing child, Riley's parents would have been less inclined to make allowances for his smearing. As an outsider, it was easier for me to see that his behaviour might be an expression of something other than a failure to understand.

Healthy aggression

Healthy aggression is a normal part of childhood development although as a culture we are not always very comfortable acknowledging this. Public images of children tend to "sanitize" them, promoting a romantic and idealistic view of childhood. Yet the ability to feel and express aggression is not only normal but also an essential ingredient for mental health. All parents are familiar with the "terrible twos" where children pit their will against that of the parents, and in the course of those struggles develop a firmer and more robust sense of themselves. Later in the teenage years a similar process takes place. Such struggles are essential for the development of identity and self-esteem.

Children with special needs also need to be able to say "No" and assert themselves. At times they will express their bad feelings by lashing out at someone and like all children should receive a clear message that this is not acceptable. However, this developmental stage can be complicated for parents and children to negotiate together where there are special needs. I think there are at least two reasons for this.

First, it can be difficult to distinguish between behaviours which are passing and those which are the beginning of new and undesirable more permanent characteristics in the child. Because the disability is itself lifelong, there can be a tendency to assume that secondary behavioural difficulties are too.

> Although Jacob, who had cerebral palsy, was delayed in many areas of his development, in some important ways his development seemed to be following a normal path. Around the age of two he began to be less cooperative. He resisted going to bed at his usual time, became more actively resistant to his mother's ordinary requests for his compliance when getting dressed, and in a small playgroup he began to pull at and grab other children's hair. His mother was very alarmed by these developments. She explained that she thought life was already going to be very hard for Jacob. When he had been a lovely smiley baby, everyone had liked him. She worried he was turning into an aggressive child. In her imagination she looked into a future where he was large, angry and unmanageable. It was hard for her to think that this might be a developmental stage which had to be negotiated rather than the beginning of the end of his sweet nature.
>
> Jacob's mother also clarified for me the second factor which complicates the negotiation of aggressive impulses in a young child with special needs. She told me she worried about people looking at him differently. She too felt differently about him, more cross with him, when he made life hard with his tantrums and his "bad behaviour". She was able to say with honesty, that she thought that "It's bad enough to have special needs without being an unlikeable thug as well!"

These sort of anxieties can make it difficult to react helpfully to children's aggression. Over-reacting can be counterproductive as the child gets the idea he can be powerful without limits. Under-reacting can also be unhelpful as then the child is left unsure about the boundaries of acceptable behaviour. It is well known that a proportion of children with learning difficulties go on to develop what is known as "challenging behaviour". In teenage years this can have very tragic consequences for the child and his family and in some cases has led to the need for residential care.

Such behaviour is usually defined in terms of the risk to the child or young person and to those around him. It is thought that in some cases there is an inherent link between such challenging behaviour and learning disability. There is also evidence, however, to suggest that many children with learning disability can behave in a reasonable way given the right circumstances early on in life.

Sleep, toilet-training and playgroups are the battlegrounds where these conflicts are first enacted. Parents who are depressed, exhausted and anxious may miss important opportunities to help their child to find out what is expected of them. Parents may get into a state of mind in which everything the child does or does not do is thought about in terms of their disability. As there is no "cure" for the disability, can anything really make a difference? Such states of mind and beliefs interfere with parents' natural capacity to intervene and communicate helpfully with their child.

Sexuality and sexualized behaviour

There are similar worries for parents concerning sexuality. The teenage years are the time when they are most likely to come to the fore. Even in young children, behaviour involving sexual parts of the body can cause alarm. The sexual feelings of young children is another of society's taboos; sexual feelings and activities of adults with special needs is another. In both cases, fantasies of innocence, impotence and lack of passion are challenged by observable reality.

Observation of normally developing children shows how aware they are of their own bodies as well as their curiosity and awareness of adult sexuality and the process of reproduction. The exploration of pleasurable sexual feelings through touching and exploring sexual organs is part of normal development. It becomes cause for concern when such interests become an irresistible habit, intensely preoccupying and exercising undue power over the child's mind. Young children with special needs may have a particular vulnerability in this area because the stimulation other children get from talking, playing and relating may be less readily available to them. By contrast their own bodies and pleasurable body sensations are always available.

A child who is left too much on her own, perhaps because she appears to need no one else, and with too few resources for thinking, playing and talking may well become overly dependent on her body for pleasure. She may need help to discover other pleasures, sufficiently direct and sensory in their nature, to make an impact on her. Most importantly, she may need to be actively drawn into emotional contact with someone, so that her solitary pleasure is replaced by the pleasure inherent in live human company.

> Jeremy, aged two, was often passive and lacking in curiosity. However, he would become very excited by twisting his mother's hair around his fingers and running his hand over her legs when she was wearing tights. This excitement had a sexual dimension to it as he would rub his penis against his mother's body at such times. His mother described feeling that it was not her, but just these parts of her body that interested him. She also felt that his excitement was of a very private nature and not anything that brought them closer to each other. Patiently she redirected his attention to toys and books and avoided either over-reacting to or else totally ignoring this behaviour. In time he gave up these preoccupations and her fear that he would grow up to be a "pervert" diminished.

An undue preoccupation with sexually exciting feelings may sometimes suggest that a child is anxious and using his body to reassure himself that all is well. In that case parents might try to understand and address the anxiety itself rather than focusing too much on the sexualized behaviour itself. Changes at home or school can cause feelings of anxiety or insecurity.

Because of their increased dependency and their communication difficulties, children with special needs are particularly vulnerable to sexual abuse either by adults or other children. This possibility always has to be contemplated if a child's behaviour becomes over-sexualized and if necessary social services should be asked to undertake a specialist assessment of the risks to the child's safety.

5

Diagnosis, Testing, Treatment and Therapy

Diagnosis

Most parents of ordinarily developing babies and children are fortunate never to be on the receiving end of very bad news from professionals about their child. When a diagnosis of disability is given, however, parents are presented with information that changes everything.

Diagnosis may not only entail the naming of a condition, but also bring information about its origins, perhaps its genetic transmission or the result of accidental injury in the womb. It may also come with a prognosis, a prediction of future possibilities for the child's development. Such prognoses usually reach far into the future, indeed enveloping the child's entire lifespan. Despite many advances in our understanding, sadly some parents still report being told by professionals, "He will be a vegetable", "Her brain is like a malfunctioning computer", "Forget him, have another baby". It is not surprising that many parents feel at the point of diagnosis that they have lost their child and must instead adjust to life with a "new" child. Diagnosis is a weighty medical tool.

Diagnosis of conditions in very young babies and children has a particular difficulty attached to it. Whereas when parents have lived with puzzling difficulties for years, diagnosis may bring relief and bear out their own experience that something is wrong, when children are very young, parents may have to take in the bad news before they feel they have even experienced their child for him or herself.

Jane's parents described vividly how their early minutes with their new baby were jarringly interrupted by a nurse calling for a doctor, who took the baby away with little explanation. The nurse had noticed features of Down's syndrome. Some months later, Jane's parents could not shake off their sense of being robbed, that something was stolen from them then. As Jane's mother said, "We were getting to know our baby. Then she was taken away and we had to get to know about Down's syndrome."

Scientific research provides us with increasing understanding of some conditions which it is hoped may eventually lead to prevention or cure. For this we are grateful, for of course parents need information about their child's condition. However, these matters are not simple. When a diagnosis is made, parents are confronted with the task of taking in and absorbing the information given, not only intellectually but also emotionally. The latter process may need more time than the former. Sometimes the emotional impact of diagnosis makes it impossible to take in the facts.

After a period of assessment the news was broken to Rick's parents that he had an autistic spectrum disorder. Rick's mother had attended most of the assessment appointments and she had a strong sense of his areas of difficulties. She had always found him hard to "get through to". Rick's father, however, reacted angrily, insisting the team was mistaken. His son's only problem was that he could not talk. He himself had been a late talker and his son would catch up in time. All he needed was time.

Rick's father himself needed time to absorb the diagnosis, a painful process which unfolded over the coming months. It is naive for professionals to imagine that because something has been said by the speaker, it has been taken in by the listener. In the case of Rick's father, he was able to let the team know exactly where he stood in relation to the diagnosis which made communication easier in one way.

Unlike Rick's father, some parents may be less overt about their reactions, and so more difficult to read.

Julie's parents seemed to take in the information the doctor gave them about their daughter's condition, the damage her brain had sustained and the areas of her skills which were affected. In the course of the consultation and in response to their questioning, he predicted that

walking unaided would not be a possibility for Julie. A week or so
later they talked to the physiotherapist about exercises to get Julie
walking. The physiotherapist felt concerned that they had not understood what the doctor had said.

It is a normal human reaction to try to dispose of unwanted knowledge.
Parents are faced with the task of integrating into their picture of their child,
and her future, what they are being told as "fact" by the professionals. Putting
things together in their own minds is not an easily achievable task and one
way of managing this is to keep separate compartments for separate bits of
knowledge. However, this brings its own problems. Julie's parents came into
conflict with the physiotherapist because she could not agree to the course of
therapy they wanted for their daughter.

Diagnosis, much as it may be needed and wanted, exerts another
pressure on parents which is hard to withstand. It brings the possibility of
the child being eclipsed by the condition with which they are diagnosed. In
the face of incurable disability we easily feel helpless and useless. Some
parents feel that in order to do their best for the child they must become
experts in the condition. Access to the internet opens up infinite possibilities
to read about conditions, therapies and even, it is hoped, cures. The danger
of this response is that information about the condition might begin to
replace first-hand knowledge of one particular child.

Evan's mother told me that he always seemed to have a bad day when
she herself was feeling depressed. However, she knew that didn't
mean anything – a child with his low IQ could not possibly understand what she was feeling.

None of these observations is intended to support an argument for the withholding of diagnosis. Parents of children with special needs, like all parents –
perhaps even more so – need to live with their child in a climate of well-being
and with hope for the future. The short-term impact of diagnosis on
well-being and on hopefulness should not be underestimated. Parents' natural
resilience may need extra support at times when diagnosis is made and in its
aftermath so its impact on them does not become entrenched and long term.

Testing, treatment and therapy

Some of the complexities surrounding the giving and receiving of diagnosis
are also played out in the issues of testing, treatment and therapy. Testing now

begins in the womb and some conditions can be identified early enough in pregnancy for termination of the pregnancy to be an option. These tests can also lead to interventions which make it possible to proceed with the pregnancy and birth with better outcomes for the baby.

Some tests are of course essential. It is also possible, however, to get into a frame of mind where assessing and testing become activities in their own right. This may be linked with the sense of helplessness mentioned earlier. Parents and sometimes professionals too may feel better if they are "doing something" rather than "doing nothing", that is, just being with the child in a more ordinary way.

Few parents would subject their child to tests and other interventions unless they felt it was important to do so, but worries and anxieties can interfere with the capacity to distinguish between what is really valuable and what less so. So too, in the case of therapy and treatment in general, some parents assume that "more is better" whereas this is not necessarily the case at all. In that way there can be a danger of placing themselves and their child under more pressure than is helpful. How much family time should be taken up by doing exercises prescribed as homework? While they are undoubtedly beneficial, this also has to be weighed up against all the other needs and demands of ordinary family life.

There is always a danger that parents will lose sight of the value of their own expertise when faced with professionals who offer interventions. Parents are likely to be the best judge as to how treatment can be integrated in family life.

Parents sometimes feel that unless they have tried to help their child in *every way possible*, they have failed. Yet this frame of mind may not lead to well-being within the family. Driven by the fear of being found wanting, either by others or by themselves, parents may be in danger of taking on too much.

Occasionally parents have to address directly the question of how much medical intervention should be offered to a child who has recurring episodes of illness and perhaps very long periods in hospital. Such cases are sometimes reported in the national press, usually when parents and hospital staff become embattled. All of these issues are deeply personal ones for which there is no easy answer.

It can be helpful, however, to try to understand more about the state of mind in which tests, treatments and therapy programmes are undertaken. Where there is an edge of desperation which can lead parents to try everything and always want more, it may be that this exhausting activity has the function of keeping at bay feelings of guilt, helplessness and depression. When this is the case, it is less likely there will be a good emotional outcome for the child and his family.

When financial circumstances allow it and parents are willing to embark on a family holiday with all it entails in terms of extra planning, equipment and facing the world at large, it can often be a surprise to find that their child's development does not stop or regress. The child and indeed the whole family may benefit from the new environment as well as unstructured time together.

6

Understanding Your Young Child with Autism

Autistic spectrum disorder

It does not make sense to compare one disability with another as if its impact could be weighed in a scale and found heavier or lighter. However, the potential for a young child with autism to cause great sadness and distress to his parents is undoubtedly considerable. Parents of young autistic children often go to the heart of why this is so. Some say that they don't think their child would notice if they weren't there if they died tomorrow. Others say, "I know he can hear me, but it's as if he is deaf." What they are describing is the pain of feeling that despite their love and constancy, it's as if for their child they are nothing special, they do not even exist as a person. They are useful if a hand is needed to open a door or reach for a drink, but their personhood, what makes them who they are, is not felt or acknowledged by their child with autism.

Living with this experience can be debilitating, heart-breaking. Some authors describe parents' experience of life with a child with autism as "traumatic" (Alvarez and Reid 1999, p.33). The lack of feeling loved combined with the exhaustion of trying to get through to their child and perhaps also manage his sleeping and eating troubles can be extremely debilitating.

> Ali, aged three, motored around the room knocking toys off the table top and onto the floor. He did not respond when his mother called his name to attract his attention. When she tried to make eye contact with him, he avoided this, directing his gaze in a rather glazed way, to nowhere and no one in particular. When he was handed a ball he

threw it over his head and behind him. Then he seemed to forget all about it. He didn't go to retrieve it and when his mother offered it to him again, he veered away as if oblivious. His body was like a little armoured car, his face neutral and unsmiling.

Many books have been written about autism, or the wider autistic spectrum disorder. Since the condition was first defined by Kanner in 1943, there have been many attempts to understand exactly what sort of condition it is, what causes it and what interventions are most beneficial for the children who have it. Although our understanding is still incomplete, there is general agreement that genetic factors play an important part in its causation. As yet our understanding of how environmental factors interact with these factors in each individual child is very limited. It seems likely that many different combinations of causal factors may result in the spectrum of autistic disorders.

Different parents give varying accounts of their child's autism. Some will say that from the beginning of their baby's life they knew something was wrong. The baby was hard to settle; she showed little appetite for suckling and was difficult to feed; she was hard to comfort, restless and agitated and she seemed happier to be left alone in her cot than to be picked up and held.

A first-time parent may find it difficult to know whether this "strangeness" is common to all babies. An experienced parent may attribute the behaviour to this particular baby's personality and character and it is only with the benefit of hindsight that these difficulties come to be understood in a different way.

Other parents' stories are very different. Some describe how their child seemed to be developing normally for the first year. He may even have been babbling and pointing in a communicative way. Yet at some time in the second year there was a deterioration. He stopped babbling and smiling, seeming to lose interest in the world around him.

Parents go over these stories many times in an attempt to find meaning in their experience.

Whatever the cause of the difficulties, their manifestation in the life of the child is profound. It is not uncommon to hear parents express the view, especially in the early years, that the autism is immutable, as if it is a heavy truck which mows down everything in its path. Perhaps this is because the condition itself is usually characterized as "lifelong". It may also be linked to its nature as a condition which easily can make parents feel depersonalised and redundant. Such feelings of fatalism and despair do not support parents in their capacity to relate to and influence their child's development.

Children who are diagnosed as having an autistic spectrum disorder have in common with each other difficulties with being sociable and communicating, whether by words or by gesture as well as difficulties in playing imaginatively as we saw in Ali. Toys to him were just something to be knocked down. He didn't invest the different toys with different meanings and potential. Many children also tend to get stuck in patterns of behaviour which can be more like empty, repetitive rituals, than communicative play. They can become very upset if their rituals are interrupted.

Autistic spectrum disorder and developmental processes

Although the difficulties in the areas of language, imagination and play and the tendency for repetition and rigidity, known as the "triad of impairments", is common to children on the autistic spectrum, there are great differences between individual children, which unfortunately can be easily overlooked. As one colleague said to me, "Autism itself is rather boring. It's the children I'm interested in".

As I have been maintaining throughout this book, prolonged, shocking and difficult experiences can interfere with our ability to think straight and to discriminate.

> Adam, aged three, had been very withdrawn for several months. He had attended a drop-in playgroup with his carer and was no trouble at all. He avoided the other children and ran around, showing no interest in the bikes and toys which caused occasional disputes among the other children. After a diagnosis of autism and some therapy, Adam's carer reported that she could no longer take him to the drop-in because his behaviour was so bad. He was bumping into other children and pushing them. He had started to bite them and take toys from them. The carer was very upset and saw this development as the beginning of the end of social contact for Adam with his peers.

As described in Chapter 4, in the course of ordinary development children have to explore and express a normal amount of healthy aggression in order to be psychologically well. When teeth begin to push through in a baby's mouth, experiences come to the fore which herald a new developmental stage of life. The soft and largely consonant atmosphere of the earlier months becomes more variegated. Expressions of and awareness of dissonance and strife become more common.

Normally this begins within the safe confines of the family and can be further explored in a wider social context where safety can be maintained by effective and loving adults.

> Adam, a withdrawn little boy, had up till the age of three shown no awareness of, far less feelings about, other people. He had shown little or no affection for the people who loved him. The course of his development was disordered, and yet the arrival of his biting seemed to be accompanied by a greater awareness of and connection with the world around him. It was difficult for the carer to see why this stage of development, appearing perhaps at what felt like the "wrong time" and in the "wrong place" and which certainly made her unpopular with the other adults at the playgroup, might in fact be a hopeful sign for Adam's development.

Many accounts of the nature of autism focus on the child's lack of understanding of the world around him and in particular, his lack of an understanding that people have minds. While this can be a helpful way of thinking about difficulties, there is also the question about what this little boy was *feeling*. His carer was adamant that his pushing and biting had to do with a lack of understanding rather than an excess of feeling!

When a child is diagnosed with an autistic spectrum disorder, this does not mean that his whole self is an expression of the disorder. Yet this can be very difficult to keep in mind. Family traits such as gentleness, sweetness, stubbornness or high-handedness are not obliterated by autism, and neither, thankfully, are all normal developmental impulses.

Setting limits for the young child with autism

I am grateful to the parents who have been able to explain to me their dilemma and difficulties about setting helpful limits for their young child with autism. These limits can be in relation to several areas of family life. Two of the most common are feeding and sleeping. Through conversations with these parents I have understood more about their beliefs in relation to their child and how in some very central aspects, these beliefs are at odds with other ideas and experiences.

The central dilemma seems to go something like this:

> My child is three but he is still not talking. When he wakes up at night crying, I have no way of knowing what is wrong. He may be

hungry, he may be in pain, he may really need to see that I am there for him, or, he may just feel like some company and is waking me up so I can provide it. Because he is autistic, he can't tell me what he wants or feels, and so I must not run the risk of ignoring a very real need. Therefore I allow him to sleep in my bed/next to me/in my room and when he wakes I hold him/offer him food/comfort him. The argument continues: when he is older and starts to talk, he will be able to tell me what is the matter and then I will be able to judge how to respond to him.

A similar situation can easily arise in relation to eating. The child does not eat at breakfast time, but an hour later he takes his mother's hand, pulls her to the kitchen and stares at the biscuit cupboard, giving a little hop and perhaps pinching her leg. His mother gives him a biscuit because he did not eat any breakfast. A little later this is repeated and she gives him a biscuit because he has not had a proper meal yet. An hour later, when it is lunchtime, he will not eat the meal she has prepared. This goes on through the day and when he awakes crying at 2 a.m., she thinks he may be now be really hungry because he has not eaten well all day. She goes to him and gives him something to eat.

Even for parents of children who do not have special needs or a communication disorder, saying "No" and establishing routines can be difficult. Parents have to feel secure enough not to mind being temporarily unpopular while at the same time being in touch with their child's sadness or distress. When a young child has no language and in some ways seems both mysteriously distant and yet also very vulnerable, it is hard to have confidence that it is not cruel to say "No".

One mother said to me, "I am becoming his slave."

Often parents tell me about "waiting for the child to learn to talk" or "waiting for the child to be ready to sleep in his own room". Many mothers tell me that once the child is sleeping through the night, they will feel able to put him in his own room. For the time being he will sleep in mother's bed and when he wakes, she will reach for him. It is not difficult to see then how a situation easily becomes circular.

From a developmental point of view, children need to receive from their parents a very clear message about what is expected of them. This little boy seemed to get the message from his mother that food was endlessly available, as indeed was she. If he wanted her in the night, she would be there.

I would not suggest that all children, regardless of their area of vulnerability and special need, will definitely respond in a positive way to their parents' expectations that they should sleep through the night and eat at mealtimes. There always needs to be consideration given to the child's physical, psychological and sensory vulnerabilities. However, unless parents do have such expectations, the child has too big a developmental job to try to initiate these steps on their own.

From a psychoanalytic viewpoint, in fact, waiting for the child to communicate better before setting limits on behaviour is to put the cart before the horse. There are many examples of times when it is the setting of limits which facilitates the development of communication in the child – not the other way round.

To approach this from another angle, a French psychoanalyst, Graciela Crespin, has pointed out that to parent a young child with autism, it is essential that the *parent* has a theory of mind in relation to their child (Acquarone 2007). That is to say, the parent must be able to hold on to the idea that there is a capacity in the child to understand and to relate, however impaired. With no expectations, there will be little hope of the child rising to any.

7

Play and Talking

Playing

Play is children's work and not merely a way of passing time when nothing of importance is happening. Because play is inherently pleasurable, it is an invaluable tool for learning in the very broadest sense of that term. A child with special needs is no different from any other child in this area of experience, although there may be less scope for a variety of play. It may also take longer for play to develop and more patience to discover what play is possible and enjoyable for her.

The developmental importance of play can sometimes be overlooked when a child has a disability. She may have to attend treatment sessions and undergo investigations and interventions, all of which of course may be necessary for her well-being. However, skilful clinicians, like skilful teachers, will always bring playful elements such as humour, space for diversions and the ability to relate to the child on his level and not as "an expert" into their work. Too much effort with not enough pleasurable human contact can be counter-productive for adults and children alike.

Developmental psychologists stress the importance of pleasure and joy for child development (Acquarone 2007). Parents have to be sufficiently confident in the importance of pleasurable play, as well as emotionally available, to create a space for it in their relationship with their child. This does not of course necessarily mean setting aside time ring-fenced for play. Play often erupts spontaneously in the course of ordinary life. Changing a nappy can lead naturally to a peekaboo game; bathtime can elicit babbling sounds from a child which might lead to a to-and-fro vocal exchange or just the sheer pleasure of hearing a voice in the flattering bathroom acoustics.

For many reasons, it can be difficult for parents of young children with special needs to avoid trying to make play educational. Sometimes parents feel everything has to be work. This may be linked to guilty feelings. Paradoxically play is likely to be most educational when it is least intended to be, that is, when it is most spontaneous and fun. Like jazz, it isn't a scripted activity. Children are quick to pick up on when they are being offered a play space and when they are being set a task involving colourful toys!

Play can take many forms. Noticing the right level of play for your child is important.

> William is a little boy of three with physical and learning disabilities. In the playroom his gaze focuses on a see-through cone with small animals inside that go round when you push a button on the top, a toy designed for babies. His mother notices his interest and is pleased to see it. She pushes the button and they both watch the animals go around. When they stop, his mother waits. After a pause, a little facial gesture of William's is interpreted by his mother as a request for her to push the button again, which she does. When it has stopped, again she waits. This time, William swings his feet to signal that he wants his mother to push the button again. When she does so, he smiles at her. She is delighted. Throughout, she is commenting on the process and responsive to his small cues. Equally importantly, she leaves plenty of time and space for them so that he has an important role in getting the animals moving again each time. The play brings them together. After a few runs of this, William begins to make little vocal sounds which have a friendly, conversational quality. When he begins to lose interest, he shows this by turning his gaze away from the toy. His mother is sensitive to this and waits without making further demands on him.

William's mother was prepared and able to focus on what was capturing his attention at that moment. This is a good starting point for play. Sara's mother was also able to do this.

> Sara, aged two, a little girl on the autistic spectrum, picks up the baby doll. Her mother is delighted and talks about the baby girl. "Give her a cuddle, give her the bottle." Sara tips the doll back so that her eyes close. She puts her finger into the doll's eyes. Then she sits the doll up so the eyes open again. She doesn't seem to be thinking about the doll as a "pretend baby" but she is noticing and processing something

about the eyes being open and then closed. Sara's mother wrestles with her own disappointment. She had felt so excited when Sara seemed interested in the doll, but then was actually only interested in the eyes. Adjusting her own focus she talks to Sara about the eyes which open and close, open and close just like hers. Sara takes the doll and puts it in her mother's lap.

As I have described earlier (on pages 26–7), researchers have studied family videos of twins, one of whom went on to receive a diagnosis of autistic spectrum disorder. By analysing the videos in detail they could see subtle differences in the way that each twin related to their parents' playful overtures (Acquarone 2007). As would be expected the parent and baby who went on to get a diagnosis of autism were less well synchronized and attuned than the parent with the other twin. Without any conscious thought process on the part of the parents, they automatically adjusted their playfulness when interacting with the baby with difficulties. This was partly an unconscious adjustment to suit their sense of what the baby could tolerate and enjoy. However, it also led to a situation where the twin with difficulties did not have as many successful play interactions with their parents as did the other twin. They missed out twice over (Acquarone 2007).

Communicating and talking

Communication, language and speech tend to be talked about as if they are one thing, although communicative speech is actually the result of a developmental process which begins long before speech is a possibility for the child. Parents long to hear their child speak and first words are often remembered with pride and affection. When two or three word phrases start to give way to sentences, it can feel as if children have at last found a place in the social world. Language offers a bridge between the private experience of individuals. It is a relief to feel that children can let you know about what happens when you have not been with them.

A long wait for speech to develop can be discouraging. The parents of children with delayed language development may find it hard to believe that language will ever come and find it difficult to value their child's non-verbal communication, which is after all the foundation for the words to follow.

One mother told me how she longed for her child to be able to communicate but feared that he would never be able to because of the brain injury he had received at birth. Her twelve-month-old son moaned and complained, trying to reach a toy car which had rolled under her chair. He tugged her skirt hem, screwing up his face with displeasure.

"But he *is* communicating," said father. "What's the matter, Jake, can't you reach your car?"

Such examples of successful non-verbal communication, easily taken for granted, in fact form the bedrock of speech in normal development. While in the case of children with special needs they do not guarantee that speech will develop, it is clear that meaningful speech will not be able to develop without them.

As discussed in Chapter 1, hundreds of thousands of communicative exchanges take place between parent and child long before speech develops, rooted in the inherently emotional relationship between parent and child. Researchers who study these non-verbal "proto-conversations" can identify them taking place when normal infants are just a few hours and days old. One researcher emphasizes the intimacy of the shared timing and musical phrasing of these proto-conversations (Trevarthen 2002). Another, Jerome Brunner, suggests that a game such as peekaboo allows babies to develop thinking skills, particularly in relation to understanding rules, which are then applied in language usage (Brunner and Sherwood 1975).

Without going through these stages of non-verbal exchanges, speech, even if words developed, would not be genuinely communicative. It is important therefore not to underestimate the importance of these pre-speech exchanges and not to despair when words take longer to appear than normal.

For young children sign language such as Makaton® or the use of PECS, the Picture Exchange Communication System, can be helpful as a way of getting a two-way communicative exchange going between child and adult. It helps the child get the feel of the potency of language. Parents sometimes fear that the introduction of these tools mean that therapists have given up on the idea of the child talking. However, this is not the case. They can kick-start communication which in turn may lead to speech. Sadly, in some cases children with special needs do not ever manage to use spoken words to express themselves even though they are motivated to communicate. Speech and language therapists can help with this in some cases. They are expert in the area of "assistive communication" when a child has the ability to communicate but not the physical capability of speaking in words. Older children may be helped by computer software to make themselves understood despite not being able to use their own voices for speech.

It is more problematic in some ways when not only speech but also communication is lacking. This is the situation with many young autistic children, who seem to lack an inherent interest in communication. When this is the case it is helpful to find some small way of getting a to-and-fro going with the child. Following the focus of the child's interest, as Sara's mother did, is a good way of beginning. Music therapy is another means of making contact with children who seem uninterested or unaware of the potential for communicative links with other people. In many ways, music therapy works on the principles of pre-verbal communication. The American psychoanalyst Steven Knoblauch was initially a jazz musician, and has written an unusual book about his work with adult patients. He shows the important contribution of the non-verbal aspects of communication as mediators of emotional communication even when complex verbal exchanges are taking place between adults (Knoblauch 2000). The journey from wordless to verbal communication goes at different rates for different children.

> When I first met Colin, aged two, he had no words and had a diagnosis of autistic spectrum disorder. His mother explained that unless and until he could speak, she would never be able to leave him with someone else. She thought it likely that he never would. Three and a half years later, with much psychological work achieved, she took a short and much needed holiday with friends and left Colin with his sister and father. When she phoned from abroad, Colin asked her questions and listened apparently thoughtfully to her answers. She was tremendously proud of his progress and undaunted by the gap between his chronological age and his language abilities.

With the benefit of hindsight it is easy to say that Colin's mother need not have feared that he would be mute. Without this benefit she had to stay sufficiently hopeful in the months and years he was not talking, to support his emerging communication skills. She had to perform the difficult psychological task articulated by the psychoanalyst Joan Raphael-Leff as "Not to expect too much and not to cease to expect" (PREAUT Conference, London, July 2005).

Parents, Couples and Families

Families

Families are much more than the sum of the individuals within them. In families where there is a young child with special needs, it is not possible to disentangle the elements of family life which are to do with having a child with special needs from those that are to do with the parents' own backgrounds and beliefs, their relationship as a couple, the birth order of the children, the personalities of family members and so on.

However, it is possible to get to know individual families and listen to what they have to say about their experience. In this way some themes may be discerned in stories of family life with a child with special needs.

The child with special needs cannot be understood or thought about in isolation, as if she were not part of a culture, a family, someone's child, grandchild, niece or sister. An emotional journey begins for family members when a child is born with or diagnosed with special needs. In a healthy family this journey involves everyone. Problems occur when no such journey takes place, or some people move forward while others are left behind.

Individual parents of course vary greatly in terms of how they manage the unforeseen challenges of life with a child with special needs. Each brings to the new situation their personal history as well as their current resources and areas of vulnerability. A very sporty father might be particularly devastated to learn of his son's profound physical disability. He might also be exceptionally creative in helping his son enjoy outdoor physical experiences as fully as possible.

In our multicultural society we are also learning that cultural issues too have an important role to play. In certain cultures, for example, an additional dimension of meaning is attached to the more universal sadness of having an unmarriageable daughter. In others, disability may be seen as a "gift from God", a view which may impact in many ways on parents' day-to-day life with the child. In my experience it is always helpful to take the trouble to hear from individual families what are the pressing issues for them rather than assume that they will fit into a general picture.

Stresses on parents and couples

Fathers have a central role to play in supporting mothers as they care for children and in offering the baby a relationship which contrasts with what the mother offers. Observation of infants shows that very early on in life they are aware of the inherent differences between fathers' and mothers' bodies, voices and modes of relating. These inherent differences can offer the baby a rich experience which supports his emotional and cognitive development. Where there is too much of a gap between mothers and fathers, however, this may bring difficulties not only for them but also for the child.

There are probably many reasons for the increased incidence of marital breakdown in families where there is a child with special needs than in the ordinary population. Shock, emotional strain and physical and mental exhaustion are contributing factors as are the financial pressures affecting families. Medical and therapy appointments mean someone must be available to take the child especially in the pre-school years and attempts to combine work with these commitments may increase stress levels in the family rather than reduce them.

Shared but often unspoken worries about the root cause of the child's difficulties as well as about the future can be powerful factors in the psychological life of a family.

> Mohammed's parents' marriage was placed under great strain when the extent of his developmental problems was revealed over the first few months of his life. His father was pressurized by his own parents to leave his wife and start a family with a new one. His parents were sure that the mother was to blame for Mohammed's disability, although there was no medical evidence to support this. Because the couple had a strong bond, they were able to cope with this pressure

although they had to manage without the support of half of their extended family.

When a couple can share these worries openly as Mohammed's parents did, they are less likely to exert a negative influence on family life.

It is not uncommon to find that parents take up different roles in relation to the additional pressures of having a child with special needs. While this can be a useful division of labour, both from an emotional and practical point of view, if roles become too rigidly demarcated, it can also bring problems.

Linda and James both worked in the world of commerce before their first child Lawrence was born with a genetic condition which severely affected all aspects of his development. Many out-patient appointments were needed in the early months of his life. Linda did not return to work after her maternity leave was over. Her life became a round of appointments. She did not socialize with mothers in her antenatal group because she found it too painful to compare her son's physical appearance and slow development with the other children's. She said she could not bear her friends' pity, sympathy or apparent indifference to Lawrence's difficulties. James' working day was as long as ever, sometimes longer. Linda complained that not only did she attend all the appointments, but also she then had to try to explain the advice she had been given to James when he came in tired from work. She felt left alone with the burden and responsibility of her son's care. She missed the sense of competency she used to enjoy in her job. When the weekend came, she handed her son over to James and went out. James enjoyed playing with Lawrence but resisted Linda's pressure on him to do the prescribed physiotherapy exercises with him. James said the weekend was a time for relaxing and in any case Linda was the expert on the physiotherapy exercises. The three of them rarely spent time together.

It is easy to imagine how such a situation arises. Such arrangements may work well for one family, at least for a period of time, but not for another. For it is not the arrangement itself which is problematic but the spirit in which it is lived out. Linda felt isolated and resentful. James was tired from long days at work. He felt guilty and got at by Linda. Home ceased to be a refuge for him. These feelings, if left unattended, make the couple vulnerable to separation, whether actual or emotional.

Sometimes such arrangements are not the cause but the symptom of distance in the couple's relationship. Unconsciously a couple may find reasons not to spend time together which are then reinforced by the practical demands of running a family. These reasons may be deeply bound up with feelings about having produced a child with special needs. Shame and guilt, along with the urge to express anger or apportion blame, threaten to overheat exchanges between couples. Deep-rooted fears about the union that produced the child may be avoided by separate activities and emotional distance. Avoiding sexual intercourse may also present itself as a solution to the problem of emotional intimacy with a partner, but its benefits, such as they are, are gained at a high price. While these distancing methods of coping with profound worries may be functional for a while, they undermine the solidity of the foundations of a couple's long-term relationship if they become a way of life.

Single-parent families

The higher rate of marital or partnership breakdown in families where there are children with special needs naturally often results in a single parent taking most of the responsibility for the care of the child. This is often the mother. In my experience it is not uncommon to find that years later, these single parents have not remarried and continue to struggle relatively alone with the job of caring for their child. As the child with special needs grows, he may not enjoy the ordinary process of increased physical independence.

Whereas many of the parents are both dedicated and effective, there is no doubt that without a partner to share the work, the worries and the decision-making, their task can be both exhausting and lonely.

A "special needs family"

All parents cannot help but be aware of the contrasts and comparisons between their child's development and other children's development. This is the case even when no disability is part of the picture. When a child does have special needs, comparisons with normally developing children can be even more stark.

Many families react to this by withdrawing or excluding themselves from ordinary social situations. Mothers may not want to take their child to a play-group and constantly find themselves answering the perennial "How old is he?" question. Parents may not want to take their children into public places such as parks or restaurants.

One parent described jokingly how she had thought of having cards printed with information about her child's disability on it, to hand out in parks and children's playgrounds when people stare and then look away.

Sometimes parents feel it is their duty to spare other people the awkwardness of having to confront their own responses to the child with special needs. They talk of their experience of finding that friends and colleagues with ordinary children of their own sometimes seem reluctant to see them. This may be because they feel pity for their friends, awkward and unsure what to say. While all this is understandable, it can add to the isolation of the family where there is a child with special needs.

Parents also report a dilemma in relation to demands at work. While they may need time off for appointments, they do not want to be seen as shirking or asking for special consideration because of their child's difficulties. They don't want to feel that they are in some way "cashing in" on their child's difficulties. This sometimes leads parents to keeping quiet about their situation, which can in turn leave them feeling isolated and out-of-touch with colleagues.

What these parents seem to be expressing is that while they know that their family is different from many others, they do not want to be defined by their child's special needs. While they recognize the need to acknowledge and address whatever additional needs the child brings to the family, they do not want to see themselves or to be seen as "a special needs family".

Brothers and Sisters

Parents' concerns

When parents express concern about the impact of their child with special needs on his sibling, it can be helpful to take time to think with them to what extent the brother or sister is indeed having difficulties they need help with and to what extent this concern is an expression of parents' own worries. Of course the two situations may exist alongside and interact with each other. Some parents worry about what "they have done to" the ordinary sibling by foisting on the family a child with special needs. They may imagine that the sibling will, if not now, then in the future, blame them for this. Parents may be susceptible to such worries partly because they find it difficult to stop blaming themselves or each other.

The idea of the future is a potent one in these situations. Parents can rarely allow themselves the luxury of living in the present without worrying about the future when it is unlikely their child will be able to lead an independent life as an adult. There can be a range of thoughts and feelings in connection with siblings in this matter. On the one hand it is a relief to feel that there will be someone else who can take over the job of looking out for the "child" with special needs, by then grown up, after the parents' death. On the other hand, to pass this task on to another family member, knowing what is entailed, can emphasize feelings of regret and guilt.

When parents themselves feel overwhelmed by the demands on them, they may also feel overwhelmed by the idea of another child in the family having to take them over.

Alexandra's family had emerged from a long period of mourning after many medical investigations at last made possible a diagnosis of their child's disability. Her mother Sue said that she felt she had met many good people she would never have encountered if Alexandra had not been born with special needs. She hoped that Amy, Alexandra's sister, might also in the long run benefit from all that they have been through together and not feel that her sister was too heavy a burden. Perhaps when she grows up she will be a doctor.

Sue had found some peace in herself and could imagine Amy too might be able to be free of the burden of care which Alexandra's disabilities at times represented. Perhaps her thought about Amy becoming a doctor was also an expression of her residual wish for Amy to take on a helping or caring role.

Parents sometimes ask at what age brothers and sisters become aware of their sibling's special needs and when and how they should discuss this with them. Their experience of not being able to find within themselves the answer to their own question seems to mirror what they imagine is their child's ignorance of the real situation at home. It is helpful when parents feel they have enough resources inside themselves to answer questions honestly as they arise. This will include saying "I don't know" when necessary.

Children's perceptions of their siblings with special needs

In fact it seems unlikely that even very young children are not aware of their sibling's special needs, although that awareness will not come with the same breadth of understanding and emotional overlay for siblings as for the parents. Sorting out what belongs to whom is helpful. Nevertheless brothers and sisters will, from an early age and within the context of how they see their parents managing, form their own ideas about their sibling with special needs.

Love and concern

Even very small children are able to feel genuine empathy, love and concern for brothers and sisters. This may be even more marked when they perceive their limitations and vulnerabilities. When the sibling is born after the child with special needs, they will in some ways take the situation as a given. It will be all they have ever known. It may be different when a new baby brother or sister is born with special needs after the able-bodied sibling. Then the older child already looks at the new baby, as it were from the point of view of a "big boy" or "big girl". From that vantage point, they are likely to feel genuine concern as they compare their sibling's slow development with that of their friends' siblings. They may also feel concern about their parents, to whose moods and energy levels they are undoubtedly sensitive.

Rivalry and hostility

Alongside these feelings of concern may be other less comfortable feelings.

> Sally, aged five, was learning about floods at school. When her teacher asked her to write a story about a flood she wrote that if there was a flood where she lived, her brother would not be able to escape alive because he could not walk.

This topic brought her brother to the forefront of her mind along with what may be a complicated set of feelings about him and his extra difficulties. Undoubtedly she felt concern and worry, imagining his plight in such a dangerous situation. Perhaps too she allowed herself fleetingly to imagine his demise in the flood! These feelings of hostility mixed with loving ones towards siblings are part of normal development and are not particular to children who have siblings with special needs. They may be, however, more emotionally charged when the sibling has special needs. How fully can you allow yourself to know about your feelings of resentment towards someone already identified as disadvantaged and vulnerable? Yet, by virtue of these vulnerabilities, they may well take up much more time and space than is felt by a sibling to be their due.

When parents are thinking about these matters they often struggle with the same issue within themselves. If they can tolerate their own hostile and resentful feelings they are in a good position to help their children to manage theirs.

> Catherine told me with palpable relief that although her older able-bodied daughter Leanne was "a little devil" towards her and her husband, she never showed anything except goodwill towards her sibling with special needs. She was always solicitous and caring although occasionally, "quite unintentionally", a little rough. A few weeks later, I heard that this was no longer the case and that the older child had dared to talk defiantly about putting the younger one "in a coffin in the ground". This was a particularly painful remark for the

parents to bear as their child with special needs had come near to death on more than one occasion.

Catherine and her husband discussed Leanne's outburst at home. Swallowing their sense of shock and hurt, they could see that it would not be helpful to react harshly to what their daughter had said. They did not want her to "grow up a martyr to her sibling's disability".

The pressure always to be good leads neither to goodness nor to happiness. While not encouraging their daughter to be hostile towards her sibling, Catherine and her husband were able to acknowledge her feelings of fury and resentment. In turn Leanne could express these without feeling unduly guilty. Despite her parents' fear that this would lead to an escalation of bad feelings, the opposite was the case. Having the freedom to express her hostility in fact freed Leanne to be more loving to her sibling.

Imitation and over-compensation

Some parents report that maddeningly for them, their able-bodied child imitates the child with special needs, "pretending" for example that they too are unable to walk or speak clearly. Understandably, this indirect demand for yet more effort on the parents' part can be both bewildering and irritating.

One parent talked honestly about how angry this behaviour made her and how she wanted to shout at her child, "Give me a break, it's already bad enough having one child who really has special needs!" When she was able to think further about her son's behaviour, she could see that his bid for more help from her might express anxiety that he would be expected to manage independently sooner than he was ready. She could also appreciate the subtle strand of hostility that his mimicry of his young sibling conveyed. Additionally, it seemed that this strong feeling of being got at by her able-bodied son might indeed be an indication of the aggressive feelings directed to her, the mother who had presented him with this extra-needy sibling. Once she looked at the situation from his point of view she felt less resentful of his behaviour and approached it with more equanimity.

Where there is not room in the family for the expression of painful or hostile feelings, either towards parents or siblings, a child may over-compensate by taking over the caring, mothering or fathering role, stepping as it were into the parental shoes. The sibling with special needs may constantly be talked about as "the baby" and cast in the role of the helpless infant, while the older sibling sees herself as all-powerful.

Underlying this strategy may be a worry about whether the child with special needs does have the capacity to develop and whether mother and father are truly able to manage all their additional responsibilities. Such over-compensation, if too firmly entrenched and predominant as a coping mechanism, may lead to an undue sense of burden in the long term.

Different stages of development

Siblings' feelings and responses to the child with special needs will of course interplay with their own personalities as well as their stage of development. While a six-year-old may be very concerned to show her parents what a good girl she is, adolescent rebellion may feed into more negative feelings.

> Joni, aged fourteen, was brought with her young sibling with autism to a family meeting. She refused the offer of a seat and hovered resentfully at the door looking bored and disengaged. There was some discussion about her brother's difficulties, which she did not contribute to. Eventually, however, she said with feeling that it's "just so embarrassing" going anywhere with him. He climbs over people as if they are not there and everyone thinks he's "mental". Her impassioned outburst left her parents feeling guilty and concerned as well as angry with her. Later in the session, her brother climbed on to her knee and settled himself with her. She spoke to him gently and their mutual affection was touching to observe.

Children with special needs: their feelings about their able-bodied siblings

It would be unimaginative to think that many children with special needs do not also feel or have the capacity to develop feelings for their siblings, both positive and negative.

> Four-year-old Martin, with learning disabilities and with features of autism, did not seem to be paying any attention to his eight-year-old brother, Howard, who was setting out the painting materials. When the painting was under way, however, he moved closer and sneaked a sidelong look at the paper. Before anyone could stop him, he tipped the water pot over his brother's painting and ran off with a smile.

Martin's parents comforted Howard and told him that Martin didn't understand, and hadn't meant it. This put Howard in a difficult position. He felt he was being told he shouldn't be angry, in fact that he had no right to be angry, because Martin was so much less well off than he was. To the worker present it seemed obvious that Martin's action had been intentional, an expression of ordinary rivalry.

It can be a sign of developmental progress when a child who has been withdrawn behaves in such a way, because it shows the potential for an emotionally lively connection with the people around him. This is not of course to imply that such behaviour should be condoned or accepted. However, it is worthy of parents' time to give some thought to what feelings might be being communicated at such moments and how to acknowledge them.

Tim's parents were delighted when he started to vie with his able-bodied younger brother for attention. Although he did not do this until he was over five, they assured me that it "had been worth waiting for".

These feelings and behaviours may be less evident in younger children with special needs but come more into focus with time. Where siblings are very close in age, feelings can be even more intense. Twins are a particular example where when one has special needs and the other does not, feelings can run high in the family.

Leonie and her twin Carrie had been born prematurely, but whereas Carrie had developed normally Leonie was left with a severe physical disability. She was wheelchair bound and had limited use of her arms and hands. Her speech was somewhat unclear but family members could understand her.

Their parents reported that Carrie's life was becoming quite unbearable because of the way Leonie was treating her. It seemed that whenever Carrie settled to an activity, Leonie would call out asking for something to be brought to her. Sometimes she used a commanding tone of voice which infuriated them. At other times she whined her instructions in a pitiful voice which, her parents reported they were sorry to say, they found equally infuriating. It was like a constant irritation or interruption in Carrie's playtime. The twins' parents were feeling quite powerless. What seemed most difficult was the element of something quite cruel in Leonie's treatment of Carrie. It was as if she didn't want her twin sister to have a moment's peace or satisfaction but always to be reminded how much worse off she, Leonie, was. It seemed quite likely, given the strong feelings aroused in family members by this behaviour, that it was more than just a request for practical help. It was also a powerful communication of her feelings about her able-bodied sister and the contrast between them.

In case these examples seem to focus too much on difficult feelings between siblings, Zac and his brother Lucas may return to focus the potential for warmth and love in sibling relationships.

Lucas had always been protective of his younger brother, who was on the autistic spectrum, whereas Zac mainly ignored Lucas. When Zac was four their mother reported that a simple game had developed which involved them chasing each other around the flat amidst much laughter. A year later they were taking turns to use the controls to play computer games, and not long after when Lucas was crying, Zac hugged and comforted him, saying "Don't cry, Lucas, Mummy will come". Competitiveness, particularly in computer games, continued to be a feature of their relationship and their mother commented that she thought competing with Lucas stimulated Zac's development. The warmth between the brothers also remained a strong aspect of their relationship.

As for Tim's parents it had been a long wait to see these developments, but genuinely thrilling when it came.

10

"Surprised by Joy"

This book has focused on some of the important matters in the early weeks, months and years of the life of a child with special needs. While all developmental stages of life bring challenges, the task for many parents in this period is undoubtedly a daunting one. At the time when children and parents are setting out in life together, normal processes are threatened by the shock of disability and the additional tasks it brings. At the point where parents have to find many resources to bring to their young child, they may be feeling at their lowest ebb.

During this period of adjustment it is often hard for parents to appreciate themselves and the value of their own efforts. It may be easier for those around them to note their qualities.

> Sonya's mother humorously described a hectic holiday abroad in which most of the time she felt people were staring at and judging her. Near the end of the holiday, a lady approached her on the beach. She said she had been watching her with her children over the last week and just wanted to say what a lovely family they were.
>
> Sonya's mother reported this story with a wry smile as if unsure whether I could also see this "lovely family" the stranger had described. She seemed to hope that I could, but was also a little nervous that I would not! Her perception of herself and her children was changing, though her confidence in this new picture was still insecure.

Fortunately, given time and the right support, many parents rediscover, and in some cases discover for the first time, their strength and inner resources. As this happens, they may find themselves in the words of C.S. Lewis "surprised by joy" (Lewis 1998).

Parents begin to comment on their good fortune, not because they have a child with a disability, but perhaps because their child has a particular strength: he has always been a good feeder; she loves swimming; he has never been prone to chest infections. Or they feel fortunate for a reason which has nothing at all to do with disability – a new job, a house move, travel. Disability does not define them. Many parents comment that they have met people they would not otherwise have known and have come to appreciate their personal qualities or empathize with their predicaments in new ways.

Of equal importance, they discover the capacity to be surprised and delighted by their young child, by the developmental steps he takes however small, and by all that is uniquely personal to him. As these new notes sound, a sense of greater well-being comes to the fore. This sense of well-being is of central importance. It helps parents manage the challenges of everyday family life with their young child with special needs, as well as face realistically the challenges of future developmental stages.

Appendix: "Welcome to Holland"

Emily Perl Kingsley

I am often asked to describe the experience of raising a child with a disability – to try to help people who have not shared that unique experience to understand it, to imagine how it would feel. It's like this...

When you're going to have a baby, it's like planning a fabulous vacation trip – to Italy. You buy a bunch of guide books and make your wonderful plans. The Coliseum. The Michelangelo David. The gondolas in Venice. You may learn some handy phrases in Italian. It's all very exciting.

After months of eager anticipation, the day finally arrives. You pack your bags and off you go. Several hours later, the plane lands. The stewardess comes in and says, "Welcome to Holland."

"*Holland*?!?" you say. "What do you mean Holland?? I signed up for Italy! I'm supposed to be in Italy. All my life I've dreamed of going to Italy."

But there's been a change in the flight plan. They've landed in Holland and there you must stay.

The important thing is that they haven't taken you to a horrible, disgusting, filthy place, full of pestilence, famine and disease. It's just a different place.

So you must go out and buy new guide books. And you must learn a whole new language. And you will meet a whole new group of people you would never have met.

It's just a *different* place. It's slower-paced than Italy, less flashy than Italy. But after you've been there for a while and you catch your breath, you look around...and you begin to notice that Holland has windmills...and Holland has tulips. Holland even has Rembrandts.

But everyone you know is busy coming and going from Italy...and they're all bragging about what a wonderful time they had there. And for the rest of your life, you will say "Yes, that's where I was supposed to go. That's what I had planned."

And the pain of that will never, ever, ever, *ever* go away...because the loss of that dream is a very very significant loss.

But...if you spend your life mourning the fact that you didn't get to Italy, you may never be free to enjoy the very special, the very lovely things...about Holland.

References

Acquarone, S. (ed.) (2007) *Signs of Autism in Infants: Recognition and Early Intervention.* London: Karnac.

Alvarez, A. and Reid, S. (1999) *Autism and Personality.* London: Routledge.

Bion, W.R. (1984) *Learning from Experience.* London: Karnac.

Brunner, J.S. and Sherwood, V. (1975) "Peekaboo and the Learning of Rule Structures." In J.S. Brunner, A. Jolly and K. Sylva (eds) *Play: Its Role in Development and Evolution.* London: Penguin.

Gerhardt, S. (2004) *Why Love Matters: How Affection Shapes a Baby's Brain.* London: Routledge.

Kingsley, E.P. (1987) "Welcome to Holland."

Knoblauch, S.H. (2000) *The Musical Edge of Therapeutic Dialogue.* Hillsdale, NJ: Analytic Press.

Lewis, C.S. (1998) *Surprised by Joy.* London: Fontana.

Macfarlane, A. (1977) *The Psychology of Childbirth.* London: Fontana.

Sinason, V. (1993) *Understanding Your Handicapped Child.* London: Tavistock.

Stern, D. (1977) *The First Relationship: Infant and Mother.* London: Open Books.

Stoller, R.J. (1985) *Observing the Erotic Imagination.* New Haven, CT: Yale University Press.

Trevarthen, C. (2002) "Origins of Musical Identity: Evidence from Infancy for Musical Social Awareness." In R.A.R. MacDonald, D.J. Hargreaves and D. Miell (eds) *Musical Identities.* Oxford: Oxford University Press.

Wahlberg, V., Alfonso, D. and Persson, B. (1992) "A Retrospective Comparative Study Using the Kangaroo Method as a Complement to Standard Incubator Care." *European Journal of Public Health* 2, 1, 34–7.

Further Reading

Brafman, A.H. (2004) *Can You Help Me? A Guide for Parents*. London: Karnac.

Dale, N. (1996) *Working with Families of Children with Special Needs*. London: Routledge.

Dickinson, P. and Hannah, L. (1998) *It Can Get Better: Dealing with Common Behaviour Problems in Young Autistic Children*. London: National Autistic Society.

Frith, U. (1989) *Autism: Exploring the Enigma*. Oxford: Blackwell.

Hames, A. and McCaffrey, M. (eds) (2005) *Special Brothers and Sisters: Stories and Tips for Siblings of Children with Special Needs, Disability or Serious Illness*. London: Jessica Kingsley Publishers.

Holt, G., Gratsa, A., Bouras, N., Joyce, T., Spiller, M.J. and Hardy, S. (eds) (2004) *Guide to Mental Health for Families and Carers of People with Intellectual Disabilities*. London: Jessica Kingsley Publishers.

Middleton, L. (1992) *Children First: Working with Children and Disability*. Birmingham: Venture.

Moore, C. (2004) *George and Sam*. London: Viking.

Trevarthen, C., Robarts, J., Papoudi, D. and Aitken, K. (1998) *Children with Autism: Diagnosis and Intervention to Meet their Needs*, 2nd edn. London: Jessica Kingsley Publishers.

Helpful Organizations

UK Organizations

24 Weeks Plus
twenty4weeksplus@aol.com
twentyfourweeksplus@hotmail.com
www.24weeksplus.com
Advice and support for the families of premature babies

British Society for Music Therapy
61 Church Hill Road
East Barnet
Hertfordshire EN4 8SY
Tel: 020 8441 6226
www.bsmt.org
Information about music therapy

Contact a Family
209–211 City Road
London EC1V 1JN
Tel: 020 7608 8700
Helpline: 0808 808 3555
www.cafamily.org.uk
Advice, information and support for the parents of children with disabilities

Down's Syndrome Association
Langdon Down Centre
2a Langdon Park
Teddington TW11 9PS
Tel: 0845 230 0372
www.downs-syndrome.org.uk
Helps people with Down's syndrome to lead full and active lives

Mencap
123 Golden Lane
London EC1Y ORT
Tel: 020 7454 0454
Learning Disability Helpline: 0808 808 1111
www.mencap.org.uk
Helps people with a learning disability and their families and carers

National Autistic Society
393 City Road
London EC1V 1NG
Tel: 020 7833 2299
Helpline: 0845 070 4004
www.nas.org.uk
Champions the rights and interests of all people with autism

Scope
PO Box 833
Milton Keynes MK12 5NY
Tel: 0808 800 3333
www.scope.org.uk
Advice, information and support for people with cerebral palsy and their families

Sibs
Meadowfield
Oxenhope
West Yorkshire BD22 9JD
Information line: 01535 645453
www.sibs.org.uk
Helps to make a positive difference to the lives of siblings, making growing up
with someone with special needs easier

"Unique" Rare Chromosome Disorder Group
PO Box 2189
Caterham
Surrey CR3 5GN
Tel: 01883 330766
www.rarechromo.org
Information and support for families and individuals affected by any rare chromosome disorder and for the professionals who work with them

US Organizations

Autism Society of America (ASA)
7910 Woodmont Avenue
Suite 300
Bethesda, MD 20814-3067
Tel: 301 657 0881 or 1 800 3AUTISM (1 800 328 8476)
www.autism-society.org
Raises and allocates funds to address the many unanswered questions about autism

National Organization for Rare Disorders (NORD)
55 Kenosia Avenue
PO Box 1968
Danbury, CT 06813-1968
Tel: 203 744 0100
Tollfree: 800 999 6673
www.rarediseases.org
Provides information about rare diseases and disorders

National Down Syndrome Congress (NDSC)
1370 Center Drive
Suite 102
Atlanta, GA 30338
Tel: 800 232 NDSC (6372)
www.ndsccenter.org
National parent-led organization promoting accessibility for people with Down Syndrome

Parent to Parent USA (P2P USA)
www.p2pusa.org
Provides emotional support and information for families of children with special needs

Index

Acquarone, S. 26–7, 50, 51, 53
aggressive behaviours 36–8
  see also resentment, feelings of
Alfonso, D. 19
Alvarez, A. 45
anger
  parents 59
  see also resentment feelings
assessment procedures 42–4
"assistive communication" 54–5
autistic spectrum disorders 26–7, 45–50
  causal factors 46
  child characteristics 47
  child development stages 47–8, 65–6, 67
  early manifestation patterns 46
  parent's feelings 45–6
  parent's responsiveness 26–7, 53
  play patterns 53
  sibling reactions 65–6, 67
  sleep problems 29–30

babysitters 31
behaviour patterns
  importance of early interventions 27
  see also challenging behaviours; child development
Bion, W. 19
birth experiences 17–18
biting 47–8
blame 59
  cultural beliefs 57–8
blindness, communication methods 24–5
bonding see empathy; parent–child interactions
boundary-setting
  for aggressive behaviours 36–8
  for autistic children 48–50
  for sexualized behaviours 38–9
  for soiling behaviours 35–6
brain development, effects of cortisol 25–6
Brunner, J.S. 54

care arrangements
  babysitters 31
  future concerns 61–2
  playgroups 32
cerebral palsy
  aggressive behaviours 37
  difficulties calming babies 26
  sleep problems 29
challenging behaviours 37–8
  and learning disability 38
child development 35–6, 69
  in autistic children 47–8, 65–6, 67
  importance of boundary-setting 49–50
  importance of early interventions 27
  importance of play 51–2, 67
communication issues
  baby–parent pre-verbal exchanges 22–3, 26
    and autism 26–7
    and cerebral palsy 26
  delayed development 53–5
  finding alternative strategies 24
  and games 54
  and music therapy 55
  non-verbal 53–4
  support for parents 26
confidence issues
  feelings of achievement 68
  feelings of inadequacy 24–5
  professional vs. parents' expertise 43
conflicts
  child–parents 36–8
  professionals–parents 43
coping mechanisms, parents 20–1, 24, 56–7
Crespin, Graciela 50
crying
  at night 29
  and holding 21
cultural issues 57
  blame reactions 57–8